Tulika

# JALEBI CURLS

# घुँघराली जलेबी

by NIVEDITHA SUBRAMANIAM
pictures KAVITA SINGH KALE
translation REKHA BHIMANI

निवेदिता सुब्रमण्यम
चित्र कविता सिंह काले
अनुवाद रेखा भिमानी

**Jalebi Curls / Ghunghraali Jalebi (English-Hindi)**

ISBN 978-81-8146-450-7

First published in India, 2008
Seventh reprint, 2024

Originally in English



Published by
Tulika Publishers, 305 Manickam Avenue, TTK Road, Alwarpet, Chennai 600 018, India
*email* reachus@tulikabooks.com *website* www.tulikabooks.com

Printed and bound by
Lokavani Southern Printers, Chennai, India

The raja dreams.

राजा देखे सपना।

The clouds part.
A jalebi moon dances.

बादल हटे।
जलेबीचाँद नाचे।

The rani sings in the garden.
Jalebis jingle in her ears.

रानी बाग में गाना गाए।
उसके कानों में जलेबियाँ छनके।

Jalebis, jalebis everywhere.

जलेबियाँ ही जलेबियाँ चारों तरफ़।

Now the raja smells them right under his nose.

अब तो उनकी खुशबू राजा के बिलकुल नाक तले।

His moustache has curled into jalebis.

उसकी मूँछें मुड़कर बन गई हैं जलेबियाँ।

His mother comes along.
What does she want?

उसकी माँ आती है।
उसे क्या चाहिए?

Son, she says,
and bites his moustache.

बेटा, वह कहती है,
और काट लेती है उसकी मूँछ।

The rani stops singing.
What does she want?

रानी गाना बंद करती है।
उसे क्या चाहिए?

Raja, she says,
and bites his moustache.

राजा, वह कहती है,
और काट लेती है उसकी मूँछ।

His daughter comes running to him.
What does she want?

उसकी बेटी दौड़कर उसके पास आती है।
उसे क्या चाहिए?

No! shouts the raja and wakes up.
What a horrible dream.

नहीं! चिल्लाता है राजा और जाग उठता है।
कैसा डरावना सपना।

Slowly he looks into the mirror.
He smiles.

वह हौले से आईने में देखता है।
वह मुस्कुराता है।

There is STILL one left.
Orange. Hot. Crisp.

अभी भी एक बची है।
केसरिया। गरम। कुरकुरी।